BLANK DRAWING

SKETCHBOOK

This book belongs to:

....

....

....

www.ingramcontent.com/pod-product-compliance
Lightning Source LLC
Chambersburg PA
CBHW081602220526
45468CB00010B/2745
9781984978998